Table of Contents

Introduction

Typical Brewday

Equipment

- The Kettle
- Heat Source
- The Bag
- Fermenting Vessel
- Thermometer
- Hydrometer

Ingredients

- Water
- Malt
- Hops
- Yeast

Adapting a Recipe

Mashing

Boiling

Cooling

Fermenting

Conditioning

Jargon List

Useful Tables

Introduction

The basic process for making beers / ales / lagers is pretty simple, with little difference between these types.

Malted barley is soaked (mashed) in hot water (called Liquor) at around 66°C. This allows enzymes within the barley to convert the starches in the barley into sugars.

The water containing these dissolved sugars and other flavours is drained from the barley and then brought to a boil. Hops are boiled in this solution (called 'Wort') to extract the flavours from the hops. The boiling also serves to sterilise the liquid, which is why beer was a healthy drink in times past, often much healthier than the water from which it was made.

After allowing the wort to cool, living yeast is added to begin the fermentation. The yeast is a wonderful beast for it will consume most of the sugars and convert them into alcohol and carbon dioxide. After a week or so fermenting, the beer is then ready for bottling or putting into casks.

In a short paragraph that is the basic process. However, as with any process / hobby there are umpteen variations and adjustments that can be considered to adjust the result such as:- the flavour, the aroma, the alcohol level, the fizziness, the clarity, the shelf life etc., etc., of our favourite drink.

The purpose of this book is not to be a full in-depth documentary of these processes. Instead I want to write a straightforward guide to the brewing of good quality beer, probably at home, on a small scale, using simple, cost effective equipment, much of which you can make or modify yourself.

A typical home brew batch size is 23 Litres (5 imp. Gallons, 6 US Gallons) and this book tends to document the procedures for that quantity.

Many recipes available in published literature on various forums of the internet aim for this as a finished volume. However, brewing twice as much or half as much is not much different and many people, I know, brew 50 litres at a time or more.

Unusually for a book of this nature, first I shall briefly document a typical, for me, brewday with a list of ingredients. This should be sufficient for the reader to follow step by step and end up with around 23 litres of good beer without any understanding of what is happening and without much explanation of the reasons for each stage.

Then, the majority of this book will go into more detail about the equipment I use and some of the alternatives used by others, the different key stages and processes from start to drinking, and some comments about the ingredients and additions.

At the end of the book is a glossary of some of the terms often used by brewers, and some useful tables.

Typical Brewday

Here's the recipe I'll work to, a simple Pale Ale with some of my favourite hops.

Fermentables for Mashing	Weight	
Pale Malt	5400 grams	
Torrefied Wheat	160 grams	
Hops for Boiling	Boil Time	Weight
Galena	90 mins	30 grams
Ahtanum	10 mins	20 grams
Mosaic	0 mins	20 grams
Final Volume:	23	Litres
Original Gravity:	1.054	
Final Gravity:	1.013	
Alcohol Content:	5.4%	ABV
Total Liquor:	33.9	Litres
Bitterness:	49	EBU
Colour:	9	EBC

08.30

Gather my burner, gas cylinder and brewing pot from the shed and set up on the patio table. Rinse the brewing pot and then start filling (Make sure the outlet tap is closed !!!). Turn on both gas rings on the burner and ignite. Once I have 30 litres in the pot, I add a level teaspoon of Gypsum and a generous pinch of Epsom salts then put the lid on and wait for it to heat to 71°C.

I know my setup will heat 30 litres of water at a rate of about 2°C per minute and the water is usually around 10°C or 12°C at this time of year. I have 30 minutes before I need to come back, time to prepare for 'mashing' and gather all the other bits I need. Mashing bag, thermometer, long stirring spoon (often called the 'Mash Paddle').

08.45

Weigh out my grains (the Grist) using the kitchen scales and a clean bucket. Digital scales are great as most of them have a 'TARE' button that will allow you to reset to zero after each ingredient is added.

Most of this is the pale malt which is known as the base malt. The wheat in the recipe helps to give the beer a good head. For a stout or porter there would be some much darker roasted malts.

09.00

I've checked the temperature of the water (the 'Strike' temperature) and it's at 71°C so I turn off the gas to the burner. I put the bag into the pot and fold the top edge of the bag over the rim of the pot and past the handles.

I start pouring in the grains, stirring them in to make sure that it is all mixed up well and there are no clumps of dry grains sticking together.

I'll spend perhaps 10 minutes doing this, pouring and stirring to make sure that every grain is wet. Once I'm happy that the 'doughing in' is finished I'll check the temperature again whilst stirring. I'm aiming for between 65°C and 67°C.

I'll put the lid on and insulate the boiler by wrapping an old coat around it and zipping up. Some people use blankets or sleeping bags or towels, maybe their coats are not as big as mine!

The aim of the insulation is to maintain the temperature in there. The mash should not really drop by more than a couple of degrees over the 75 minutes or so until you next check it.

Now, be patient. I'll go and weigh the hops into three lots, as per the recipe. After opening each bag and using what I need, I'll try and re-seal the bag as airtight as I can. Elastic bands and bulldog clips are useful here, then back into the freezer go the bags where the dark and cool will help to keep them fresh.

10.15

The mash has been going for 75 minutes and should be done now. Its time for 'mash out' in which the temperature is raised to around 76°C.

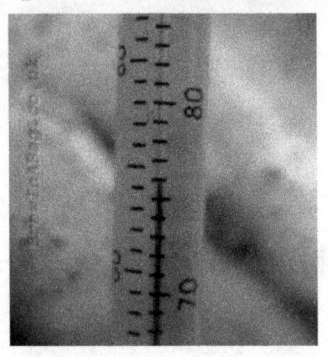

I have a hook in the roof above my boiler which allows me to lift the bag a little with a chord and pulley. This makes sure that the bag is not in contact with the base of the pot when I light the burner again. Others may have a grill in the bottom of the pot to keep the bag off the base or even a stainless steel colander.

I heat the liquid ('the Wort') and keep stirring and checking the temperature. Once I hit 76°C, off goes the gas and the bag is lowered back in, a quick stir and the lid goes on. I leave like this for around 15 minutes. At this point pretty much all the useable sugars have been extracted.

I lift the bag fully out of the pot using the chord and pulley and fix the chord. The bag will stay there now to drain its precious wort into the pot.

Meantime, I re-light both rings on the burner to bring the wort up to boiling point.

10.45

The wort has started to boil, there is a thick foam on the top surface that I skim off with a long handled spoon. The wort will be boiled for 90 minutes. As soon as it is boiling I add in the '90 minute' hops.

90 minutes of boiling will extract the oils from the hops that give the beer its bitterness and will also help preserve the beer. There will not be so much other flavour or particularly aroma from these hops as there will from the later additions. Tip them in and give a stir.

I notice that there is some cloudiness forming in the boiling wort which over a period of ten minutes or so begins to clump together, this is the 'hot break' when unwanted proteins come out of solution.

I find that of the two gas rings on my burner, one is enough to maintain a rolling boil and a 'rolling' boil is needed, a gentle simmering is not enough. I leave the lid off so that steam and gases can be carried away.

After fifteen minutes or so, most of the wort has drained out from the suspended bag of grain. I use a couple of flat saucepan lids to give it squeeze (it is too hot to do with bare hands) which gets perhaps another litre of liquid out then I remove the bag from the hook and put it in a bucket.

I know I can leave the boiler now for at least an hour, just checking occasionally to make sure it hasn't boiled over or the gas for the burner hasn't run out.

I empty the grains from the bag into the bucket. The chickens will get most of that or perhaps some of it will be made into dog biscuits for my dogs.

I turn the bag inside out, hang it on the washing line and hose it down with a cold water hose pipe then leave it to dry. It will pick up some discolouration each time it is used, particularly if dark roasted grains are used. This is not harmful or detrimental to taste of future batches.

11.55

After 80 minutes, with just 10 minutes boiling to go, I will add the 20 grams of Ahtanum '10 minute hops'. These will only be boiled for 10 minutes and so will not add much bitterness. However the flavour and aroma will be brought out of these hops in that time.

At this point I also put in the wort chiller. When cold water flows through this, it will speed up the cooling of the wort once the boil is finished. By putting it in now it will ensure that it is sterilised. Prior to boiling, things need only to be clean. Once the wort is boiled, everything it will come into contact with will need to be not just clean but also sanitised to get rid of any germs/spores/nasties.

Additionally I will put a 2 litre jug under the tap and run out some of the boiling wort then tip it back into the top of the boiler. I'll do this a couple of times. This will sanitise the tap and pipe as well as the jug, just in case there are any nasties lurking in there. I'll also drop in half a 'protafloc' tablet which will help clear the beer.

12.05

Boiling is pretty much finished. I'll add the Mosaic '0 minute' hops and stir them in, then turn off the burner. The Mosaic hops at this point will not get any real boiling action, barely any bitterness will be released but they will add flavour and aroma to the beer. I'll draw off a small amount of the wort into a tall narrow jar so that, once cooled, I can check the specific gravity.

I'll turn on the water to the chiller. The cold water going in will come out rather hot and so I catch the first 25 litres or so in a large plastic bucket that I'll use for cleaning up at the end. Once that is full the output from the chiller goes into the drain.

It takes around 30 minutes for my chiller to cool the wort down to $30°^C$. During this time I clean and sanitise my Fermentation Vessel and the lid and airlock. I put a small amount of vodka or rum in the airlock as well as drink a small sample for myself now that it is afternoon :-)

12.45

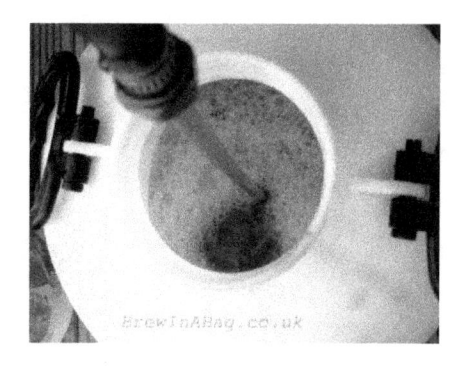

Using a sanitised thermometer I check that the temperature is below 30°C then, with the Fermentation Vessel below the tap, I let the wort flow out of the boiler.

The aim at this point is to get plenty of oxygen dissolved into the wort so I make sure there is plenty of splashing in the FV as the wort goes in, even shaking around the FV for a while until the volume of liquid becomes too heavy to do this properly.

Initially it flows pretty fast, but as we near the last few litres it slows down to little more than a trickle as the hops and 'gunge' cover the hop filter and reduce the flow. Overall it takes around 15 minutes to fill the FV.

I fit the lid and carry it indoors to a warmer room where it can stay at around 18°C - 20°C for a week or more.

13.00

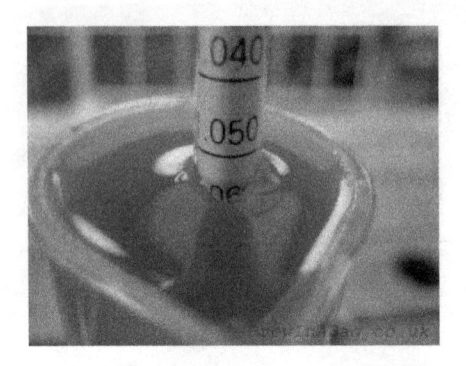

The sample I took earlier has now settled and is ready to put the hydrometer in to. I take a reading from the hydrometer and note that it just 1.052. However, checking the temperature of the sample, it is 29°C.

Correcting this for the hydrometer which is calibrated at 20°C indicates the specific Gravity is just over 1.054, which, within reason, is as expected (1.054 was the target).

I open the lid of the F.V. and sprinkle one 11.5g sachet of Safale-04 dried yeast onto the top of the wort. I can now leave the fermenting for at least a week. During the first 12 hours little happens that one can see. Usually 24 hours after sprinkling the yeast, the airlock is bubbling away nicely, perhaps one bubble every 30 seconds or so. This continues for perhaps two more days then slows down.

After a week I'll check the specific gravity every day by using a sanitized turkey baster to draw off a sample for checking with the hydrometer. I'm expecting it to get down to 1.013 and so if I get any reading below 1.015 that stays the same for more than 48 hours, then I'll know it has finished and is ready for kegging or bottling.

I spend the next 20 minutes or so cleaning up and putting things away. Carefully dispose of the hops as they are rather poisonous to dogs. Finished by 13.30, a 5 hour brewday. If time is tight, this can be reduced by an hour by only mashing for 60 minutes and only boiling for 60 minutes which some people do, reportedly with barely noticeable difference in finished product.

That pretty much completes the brief run-through of a brew-day. The time would not be significantly different if I was brewing 50 Litres, perhaps a while longer (45 mins total) to bring up to temperatures. The rest of the book now goes on to look in more detail at the equipment that can be used, what is happening during each of the main processes and discussing the main 'ingredients' of home beer making.

Equipment

Whilst it is possible to brew with less, the minimum of equipment you need to make 23 Litres of good quality craft ales and beers, using the BIAB method of 'All Grain' brewing, is as follows.

Large pot (Kettle) with tap and filter for mashing and boiling, typically 35 – 45 Litre capacity.

Suitable mesh bag to hold the grain in the pot during mashing and strong enough to lift out the wet grain, typically 10Kgs or more. Some strong handles help.

Heat source for boiling the wort, usually gas burner, kitchen cooker or electric elements in the pot.

Fermentation Vessel. Typically around 25 to 30 Litre capacity.

Thermometer capable of measuring hot liquids at up to boiling.

Bottles and caps or a suitable pressure vessel (keg) for conditioning and storing the beer.

Hydrometer for measuring the proportion of dissolved sugars in liquids.

Suitable tubing for syphoning beer into bottles or keg.

Most other bits and pieces can be found in your kitchen such as

> Scales for weighing grains and hops.
>
> Long, food-safe spoon for stirring.
>
> A jug of around 1 or 2 litres capacity.

The Kettle

Capacity

The most important piece of equipment you will need is the pot (usually called the Kettle' or the 'Copper'). This is the vessel in which you will mash your grains to extract the sugars and flavours from them and then use the same pot to bring your liquid to a rolling boil to extract flavours from the hops and drive other reactions to improve the beer.

What factors influence the size of pot needed.

- Target amount to go into the fermentation vessel (FV)
- How much liquid will be absorbed and retained by the dried hops.
- Amount lost to evaporation during boiling.
- Quantity of water absorbed by the grain
- Extra space at the top needed for stirring when 'doughing in' the grain.

The pot needs to be big enough to hold all the liquid and the grains for the mashing. Additionally there will need to be room for stirring. It is always better to get a little bigger than you think you need. Overflowing sticky wort is not pleasant and difficult to clean from most surfaces.

For BIAB one pot is used for mashing and boiling. During the process a lot of the starting water is lost. The grains will absorb and retain much of it. A good portion of the water evaporates to the atmosphere during boiling. The dried hops will retain a lot of water.

Clearly the amount of extra needed at the beginning of the process depends on how much grain will be used, how much will be boiled away and what quantity of hops are required. Through the process it would not be uncommon to loose a third of the starting water.

Most recipes you will find and most computer software will allow for what is lost during a typical brew day.

I'm always aiming for 23 litres in the fermenting vessel and so usually start with 35 litres of water in the pot. If I'm brewing a particularly strong beer, such as an Imperial Stout, which has a lot grains in the mash, then I'd start with extra water, perhaps 36 Litres.

Remember also that water expands as it is heated. Starting with 35 Litres of water at, say, 20°C, will be nearly 36.5 litres when at 100°C. My pot is 40L capacity so one can understand there is not too much spare space.

As a rule of thumb, get a pot which is at least 60% more capacity than you wish to end up with in your fermenting vessel. There are ways around this problem if, for example, you wish to brew an extra strong beer with plenty of grains, or more than your regular quantity in the fermentation vessel and I'll cover that later.

At its simplest you can use a standard pot, unmodified. After boiling and cooling, the wort, ready for fermenting, can be siphoned into the fermenting vessel.

However, your brewing day will be easier if you can fit a tap near the bottom of the pot and draw the wort from that into the fermenting vessel. This will be arranged so that after the boiling is finished and the wort has cooled, you can open the tap and allow the liquid to drain out.

On the inside of the pot you'll benefit from a hop stopper (filter). This will stop the hops from coming out through the tap and into the fermenter. If you're handy with a bit of plumbing and a drill, a simple stopper can be made with 15mm pipe, a few 90 degree elbows and a tee junction. Before soldering it all together, drill plenty of small holes for the wort to drain through.

You can buy ready made beer brewing kettles in a range of sizes complete with tap, hop stopper, level indicator, even thermometer. All these extras are nice to have but you can do very well with buying a plain pot and fitting just a tap and hop stopper yourself.

Pot Material

Stainless steel is usually the preferred metal these days. It is very hard wearing, reasonably good as a conductor of heat and generally very easy to clean. Stainless steel is quite difficult to drill as it is a fairly hard metal. This means that modifying your pot to have taps or heating elements is more difficult.

Stainless steel is also a relatively expensive metal for manufacturers to buy and to work with so overall this will be the most expensive option.

Aluminium is a very good alternative and generally cheaper. It is a better conductor of heat but being softer metal is not so resistant to damage and dents. It is very easy for drilling. It is not so easy to clean as stainless steel. It is generally much cheaper than stainless steel.

Food and temperature safe plastics are an even cheaper alternative. Obviously, these would need to be heated electrically from within by an element similar to a kitchen kettle element and indeed this is how many people brew.

My first boiler was made from a plastic fermentation vessel, with two 2kW kettle elements mounted near the base and a tap and hop filter at the front. It worked fine for a dozen or so brews but never felt totally safe as the plastic would become softer as the wort temperature reached boiling point.

Heat Source

One needs to be able to heat the water to around 66°C for the mashing and then to 100°C for boiling. The boil needs to be quite a vigorous boil, a gentle simmer is not good enough. A powerful heat source will be needed.

Gas heating

If the pot being used is metal then a gas burner, using typically Propane or Butane is very commonly used. Quite high power heaters can be bought for not a lot of money.

For my 40L aluminium pot I have a 7kW butane heater which works really very well.

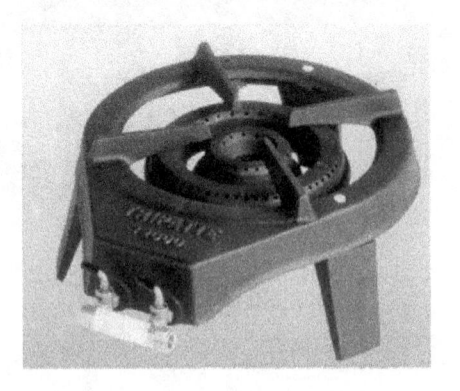

In the UK, and I guess many other countries, these are available from camping shops, home brew shops, catering suppliers, etc., and can be easily found on-line also, e-bay, Amazon, the usual places.

You'll also need a cylinder of gas, a regulator and some suitable tube to connect together.

I always brew outdoors, on the patio, protected from the rain (I'm in England) by a sloping roof but no sides. With gas heating outdoors it can help to have some shield from the effects of wind. It is surprising how much heat can get carried away by a light breeze. I have a thin sheet of steel which wraps around the burner and the pot, perhaps 5cm away all round.

Burning Butane and Propane (or any other gases) gives off some poisonous fumes such as carbon monoxide and so this fuel must be used in a well ventilated area. If you're brewing in your garage, you'll need to keep the door open for example.

Electric heating

Electric heating elements have some advantages and disadvantages. There are no poisonous fumes so using in a confined space such as a garage or shed or conservatory is no problem.

The boiling pot can be insulated round the outside and the bottom. This reduces the heating time and will often allow just one 2kW element to maintain a rolling boil.

My first boiler was constructed in this way. There were two kettle elements, each 2kW, taken from dismantled kettles from the local supermarket 'value' range at approx £5 each. Both elements would be powered on to bring the wort up to boiling.

Once boiling I would switch of one element. The outside of the pot was insulated with a synthetic foam cut from a camping mattress.

Unlike using a gas cylinder, your electricity is unlikely to run out half way through a boil saving an urgent trip to the local gas supplier. Electric boiling is also rather efficient in that all the energy going into the element is converted into heat energy in the wort itself. With gas heating, a significant portion of the heat energy never gets into the wort and directly heats the surrounding air.

In the UK, the high price of cylinder gas makes the cost per unit of heat not much different to electric heating, whereas I understand the price of butane/propane is much, much cheaper in USA for example making gas fired boiling almost universal.

Using electric elements in the boiling pot is also space efficient, there is no need to store a gas cylinder and burner equipment. This is quite an important consideration for those with smaller accommodation and more limited storage space. For many brewers living in apartment blocks or other similar places without an outside working area, then electric element heated boiler may be the only viable option.

There are also disadvantages though to electric element heating. Generally it makes cleaning up more difficult as one has to clean around the element.

If the element is small, then the heat density will be high. The transfer of heat from the source into the liquid will be done over a very small area (the surface area of the element).

With gas heating, the surface area of the whole base of the pot is where the heat is transferred. This is not a huge issue but many have found that the elements themselves become coated in a layer of burned on malt during the boil, particularly when boiling a high gravity ale and using some of the darker malts.

Cleaning up afterwards is more difficult when having to clean the complex shape of some electric elements.

Commercially available water boilers (Tea Urns in England) are available and very suitable with hardly any modification.

Some of these have a 'hidden element' that is built into a flat surfaced disc which itself forms the base of the pot. Search on e-bay for 'Buffalo' boiler to find such examples although there are other manufacturers of similar boilers such as Burco.

If you are going to use an electrically heated boiler that you make yourself, then be sure to get a competent electrician to check and install the elements and wiring.

Also one should consider just how much current is safe to draw from the wall socket in your home. This varies considerably between countries.

In North America where the standard wall socket is only 110v it is unlikely that sufficient current will be safely available to power a 4kw boiler.

Even in UK where 13 amps is usually available at the wall socket at 230v this will only be sufficient to safely power 3kW of boiler element.

Kitchen Cooker / Range

Smaller batches can be done on the home range. Typically European gas cookers will have around 1.8kW gas burners, sometimes with a 3kW burner as well.

A 3kW burner would be fine for smaller batches, up to around 20L boiling. Another important consideration when using a home gas cooker is the weight.

Not all cookers are built strong enough for 35 litres of liquid, 5Kgs of grain and the weight of pot, tap, filter and lid.

A further disadvantage of brewing indoors on a domestic cooker is the amount of steam that is generated and dispersed around the kitchen and surrounding rooms by boiling sizable quantities of liquid for an hour or more.

Whilst many consider the aroma of boiling wort and hops to be heavenly, it is not always considered to be so by all occupants of the household.

The Bag

After mashing the grains in water for 90 minutes or so, the grain needs to be separated from the wort. More traditional, 3 vessel brewing methods would drain the wort off through a tap in the bottom of the 'mash tun' and into the boiler and use a process called 'sparging'. That operation used to take me typically 45 minutes if it went well.

Here though is one of the big benefits of the BIAB method. The grains are in a porous bag that is in the liquid. To separate the spent grain from the sweet wort is simply a matter of lifting out the bag that contains the grain.

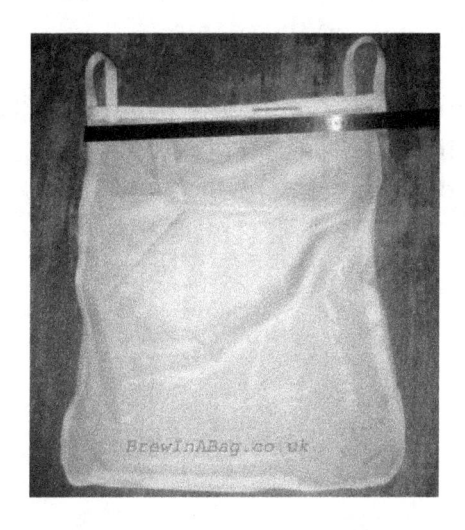

The bag needs to be wide enough to go over the rim of your pot. Measure the circumference of your pot with a flexible tape measure (sewing tape measure for example) or measure the diameter with a ruler and multiply by Pi (3.142, remember from school!).

The width of the bag, when flat, needs to be at least half of the circumference of the pot. If you want the bag to go over the handles of the pot as well then add on a suitable amount for that.

Clearly the bag needs to be strong enough to hold the wet grain which could easily be four times the weight of the dry grain when it is first lifted out.

Generally the weak points of any mashing bag are the seams so check that there is good reinforcing around the seams.

Lifting the heavy bag of wet grains will be made easier if the bag has at least two handles to get a proper hold of during the lift.

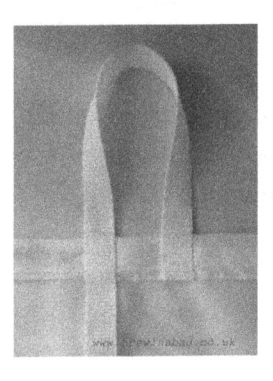

Many home brewers will have a simple pulley above the brewing pot, with a chord passed over the pulley to a hook. This can be hooked into the handles to make lifting the bag out easier.

Additionally, by tying off the chord, the bag can then be allowed to hang over the pot for 30 minutes or so to drain the precious wort out.

The fabric from which the bag is made needs to be chosen carefully. Commonly the materials used are either polyester or nylon.

Polyester has a slightly higher melting point than nylon and is a little more durable. The bag should not come into contact with any hot electric element for heating or with the base of the pan if the heat is external.

The mesh size is not critical but bare in mind that a larger mesh will let bigger particles of grain pass through whereas a smaller mesh may take longer to drain.

Both polyester and nylon are easily cleaned and resistant to mould. I clean my bag with a water jet from the hose and hang on the washing line.

A well made, good quality bag should last for very many brews. I've been using one now for three years, probably over 30 brews and looking at it, can see that it will last for many more years.

Fermenting Vessel

There are many options here. The basic requirement is for a food-safe container, with a capacity 20% more than the amount of beer you want to produce.

Whatever you use will need a lid or cover that can keep out infectious bacteria and other nasties. It will need to be able to let out the carbon dioxide gas that is produced by the yeast. Whilst a clean cloth draped over a bucket would probably do the job, best will be some vessel with an airtight lid and a way of fitting an airlock to let out the gases.

For the home-brewer a food-safe polypropylene bucket with lid, of around 30L capacity is ideal. Similarly priced (UK under £15) are purpose built polypropylene fermenting vessels, with markings on the side to indicate the level of liquid and a screw on lid. This is what I use, with the lid drilled to accept a rubber bung and airlock. The airlock has a liquid in it (I use some of my wife's Bacardi) that allows the CO_2 to bubble out and prevents infections going in.

You need to be able to thoroughly clean and sterilise the fermenting vessel before any of your valuable wort goes into it. For this reason, it is handy to be able to get your arm into it so that your hand can reach all the corners to clean properly. Having said that, most US home brewers seem to use a large glass carbouy with a very narrow neck without issue.

Going a bit more professional, there are stainless steel fermenting vessels available at considerable expense. Often, these are conically shaped with a tap at the bottom. The tap allows the used yeast to be drawn off before the beer comes out of the same tap. Most home brewers though use a syphon tube to transfer the beer from the fermenter into storage (bottles/keg/whatever).

Thermometer

An essential item for checking temperatures during mashing and also checking the wort has cooled sufficiently before pitching the yeast.

Mechanical Dial thermometer. These rely on the differing rate of expansion of different metals to move the pointer on the dial. They are rugged, accurate and reliable and used by many professional and amateur brewers. The more economically priced ones are likely to be less accurate and also perhaps more likely to loose accuracy over time. Many pre-built stainless steel boilers will be provided with one of these fitted as standard.

Glass Spirit thermometer.

Very traditional, perhaps the oldest design of thermometer. Accurate, stable and reliable.
Their weakness is their fragility, they do not take kindly to be dropped and if dropped onto a boiler of wort, you may end up with spirit and broken glass in your beer. Having said that, this is the type of thermometer that I use almost exclusively, mainly because I trust it due to it's simplicity.

Electronic digital thermometer.

Modern high tech that can be priced from a few pounds/dollars/euros up to very significant amounts. Try and get a waterproof one, generally electronics, liquids, steams do not mix very well but many people use these without issue.

Check your thermometer often against a different thermometer that you also trust. I've had a digital thermometer in the past, admittedly a low cost one, that would read 65°C when in fact the temperature was over 80°C. Mashing temperatures are quite critical to within 2°C or 3°C.

Hydrometer

Good beer can be brewed without using a hydrometer, but it is such a useful tool for monitoring your process and improving and also relatively cheap these days that no home-brewer should be without one, and possibly a spare one as well, in case.

The hydrometer is designed and constructed such that it will sink into a liquid to a certain depth. How deep it sinks depends on the density of the liquid. It is made so that in pure water it will sink to a depth where the scale reads 1.000.

The density of water will increase if sugars are dissolved in the water, the hydrometer will not sink so deep. The density of the liquid will also change with temperature. As a liquid heats up, its density decreases and the hydrometer will sink deeper.

> & WINE HYDRO
> y @ 60°/60° F.
> (15.56°/15.56°C

Hydrometers are calibrated to be accurate when the liquid is at a certain temperature. For modern hydrometers this temperature is usually $20°C/68°F$, older thermometers were typically calibrated at $15.6°C/60°F$.

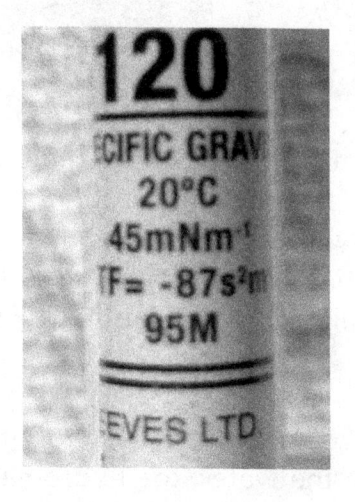

> 120
> CIFIC GRAV
> 20°C
> 45mNm^{-1}
> F= -87s^{2}m
> 95M
>
> EVES LTD

The calibration temperature should be printed on the side of the hydrometer. Measurements should be taken when the liquid is at this temperature, however, measurements can be taken at other temperatures and then an adjustment made for the temperature difference. There is a formula for this adjustment but I have included a table of adjustments at the end of this book.

The calibrations on the side of the hydrometer will indicate the density, *relative to pure water*. This is called the 'Specific Gravity' and pure water will have a specific gravity of 1.000 whereas a typical wort with the dissolved sugars from the malt may have a Specific Gravity of 1.050.

The Specific Gravity of the un-fermented wort is usually called the Original Gravity, or OG for short.

The specific gravity will be lower at the end of fermentation because the yeast will have consumed most of the sugars and converted them into alcohol. The specific gravity at the end of fermentation is called the Final Gravity, or FG for short. By knowing how much sugar has been converted it is relatively simple to calculate the approximate ABV (Alcohol By Volume) using this formula:-

ABV = (OG - FG) * 131

This approximation formula is good enough for 'typical' beers between 4% and 6%. There is a more complex formula for weak or strong beers and there are many ABV calculators on the internet where one enters the OG and the FG and the ABV will be calculated. Just search for 'ABV OG FG'.

An example:-

Measure the Original Gravity of the wort, in the fermentation vessel, at 20°C before pitching the yeast and the reading is **1.050**.

After fermentation is finished, measure the Final Gravity at 20°C and the reading is **1.012**.

Alcohol content (ABV) = (1.050 − 1.012)*131 = **4.99%**

Ingredients

Water

You'd think 'water is water' but the water that is coming out of your cold water tap varies significantly depending mainly upon where your water supplier draws their water from. The chemicals within the water have a big effect on how the sugars are extracted during mashing and also how the yeast works on these sugars during fermenting.

Municipal water suppliers will filter the water and add chemicals, such as chlorine, to help remove harmful bacteria and perhaps fluorine to help strengthen teeth.

The ground water in different areas has different quantities of residual elements in such as Calcium, Magnesium, Sodium, etc. as well as different acidity and alkalinity.

The quantities of these chemicals are usually small, measured in parts per million and are quite harmless for drinking, indeed many of them are essential for our own bodily systems.

Water supplies in Pilsen are great for producing crisp lagers. The ground water in Burton on Trent, England, was found to be just great for English bitters and pale ales.

Whole books have been written on the treatment of water for brewing and as your expertise in home brewing develops you will want to pay attention to this aspect of the hobby.

Initially though it should not concern you too much. Beers were being brewed for centuries before anyone thought about water analysis and special treatments, other than perhaps boiling the water and letting it cool before using it to brew. There are some simple steps you can take though that may help.

Hard Water

If your water supply is considered 'hard' water, you'll probably know this from the fur in your kitchen kettle, and perhaps scale around taps, difficulty making a lather from soap and other common signs. This 'hardness' is due to Calcium Bicarbonate dissolved in the water and is particularly common in chalky areas. It is often called *temporary hardness* because it is relatively easy to remove.

Calcium Bicarbonate has negative effects in the mashing process by increases the pH and reducing mash efficiency. Calcium Bicarbonate is believed to adversely affect the flavour from the hops during boiling, generating some 'harshness' in the taste. Calcium Bicarbonate is not wanted during fermentation either for its adverse effects there.

If your water is hard water then simple steps should be taken to correct this. The simplest way to remove the temporary hardness is to boil the water before brewing.

Many brewers will boil the water for 10 minutes, or so, withe the lid off the boiler, the night before brew day. The Carbonate will precipitate out of the water and then settle at the bottom of the boiler like chalk dust. In the morning, before brewing, carefully pour the water off into another container and tip away the Calcium Carbonate and rinse before re-filling and heating the water for brewing to start.

Another way to treat the water to remove this temporary hardness is to treat the water with acid. Sulphuric or hydrochloric acids are typically used. You'll need to analyse how much temporary hardness is in your water then add the right amount of acid to correct this. I shalln't go into more detail than that in this book as pre-boiling is sufficient for most brewers that have hard water.

If you're brewing a dark stout or porter, with heavily roasted malts, then a hard water is probably beneficial as the acids in the malts will counteract the alkalinity.

Chlorine

Chlorine added by the municipal water supplier is considered by some as a problem, perhaps adding a 'clinical' taste to the finished beer. I'm not convinced this is the case because during the boil any chlorine present will be driven off. However, many people still treat for chlorine.

Chlorine and Chloramine can be removed from the water before mashing by adding half a crushed Camden tablet and stirring well whilst the water is heating to strike temperature. If you're boiling your water initially to remove hardness then this will not be necessary as the boil will serve the same function.

Salts

Calcium is important for the proper function of the enzymes that convert the starch to sugars during the mash. It is also important for the proper growth of yeast cells and the clarity of the beer. If your water is very 'soft' water, you'll probably benefit from adding a little calcium to the water. This is done by adding Calcium Sulphate (more commonly known as Gypsum).

Again, I'm not going into this in depth for this book, but would just mention that I typically add a small amount, perhaps a flat, level teaspoonful to my 30L or so of water as it is heating to strike temperature.

Magnesium is another element that is needed in your brewing water. It's main benefit is as a yeast nutrient during fermentation although it helps somewhat with extraction of flavour from the hops.
It is necessary but only needed in very small quantities, perhaps 20ppm in the fermenting wort.

Magnesium is easily added using Magnesium Sulphate (more commonly known as Epsom salts) and I always add just 1/3rd of a teaspoon to my brewing water. Greater amounts may add a sour taste to the beer. Even larger amounts will act as a laxative so don't add too much.

pH Value

Liquids can be acid or alkaline. This alkalinity is measured on a scale from 1 (strong acid) to 14 (strong alkaline) with pure water being neutral at 7. The number refers to the pH value (which itself relates to the amount of available hydrogen ions).

You could check the pH value of your water, but that is, itself, not directly relevant. What is important is the pH value of the mash, when the grains are in and the enzymes are working, which should be around 5.3pH for optimum efficiency.

You can check the pH during mashing and keep a record. If it was too high or too low, then next time you make a similar beer make some adjustment to the water before the mashing. If the pH in mashing was too low then adding a little more gypsum to the water will help correct this next time.

Malt

Barley is grown in many countries. In the UK it is the second most commonly grown arable crop after wheat. It needs considerable processing to extract the sugars and goodness we want in our beer.

A big part of the work is done by the malting house that takes the harvested and dried barley from the farmer and turns it into the malted barley that we need.

Malting is the controlled germination of cereals, followed by a termination of this natural process by the application of heat. Further heat is then applied to 'cure' the grain and produce the required flavour and colour.

The maltster will soak the grain in water for a time, then bring it out into the warm air. This process will be repeated a few times over a period of two or three days. This causes the grains to germinate and begin converting the body of the grain into starches and sugars.

When the maltster decides that steeping has proceeded enough, it is then laid out, traditionally on wood floors, and germination continues with carefull control of air flow, temperature, humidity etc. This can take four to six days, depending on which type of malt is required.

When enough enzymes have developed within the grain to allow breakdown of the starches cell walls and modification, but before conversion into a food source for the new barley plant, the malt is then heated to stop further progress and dry the barley.

Heating is done in large kilns. Higher temperatures will lead to darker malts. The moisture content will drop to around 5% It is the skill and experience of the maltsters and their chosen actions which will determine the quality, colour and properties of the resulting malt.

Malted barley has the required enzymes present within it to convert the starches into sugars. These enzymes are activated by warmth and moisture during our mashing process.

Different malts have different 'strength' of enzymes as will different cereals such as wheat, rice, oats, etc. This is referred to as the *diastatic power*, the power to convert starches into sugars.

There are two main categories of barley, being two-row and six-row, related to the way the kernels grow around the stem of the barley plant.

Two row generally has preferable flavours whereas six row has a higher diastatic power. Having a higher *DP* malt allows it to successfully convert starches found in other crops that themselves have little or no DP. This would allow the use of significant quantities of adjuncts, such as un-malted rice or corn, to be used in the beer mash, generating sugars for alcohol without adding much to flavour, bud.

The base malt for most beer production you will use will likely be a pale malt. The large variety of other malts will largely determine the colour and malt flavour in the beer.

Dark, heavily roasted malts will be used in Stouts and Porters, Only the palest of malts are likely to be used in Lagers, for example.

When you are buying malts their effect on the colour of the beer will be given by the vendor. In Europe this is stated in EBC (European Brewing Convention) units, often you will also see degrees Lovibond mentioned, particularly in USA.

If you're building your own recipes you'll need to know the EBC of the malts you're thinking of using. Most beer brewing software available now already has built into its database the EBC of the different common malts.

Some of the more common fermentables:

Pale malt: Fully modified two-row barley only very lightly kilned. Commonly used as a base malt Intended for English-style ales, particularly IPA, ESB, and bitters. EBC usually low, around 5.

Caramel/Crystal malts: Caramel malts will have been germinated and left to allow the enzymes to convert the starches to sugars before being kilned and caramelised. Caramel malts add sweetness, perhaps a toffee flavour to your beer which can help balance a strongly bittered ale. Caramel malts include Cara-Munich, Cara-malt, Special B, Carastan. The temperature at which the malt is kilned will determine the colour and so colour can be Light ~60EBC, Normal ~150EBC or Dark ~300EBC

Munich malt: Fully modified six-row barley. Used to increase malt flavor in relation to hoppiness in dark beers, particularly Bock, Porter and Oktoberfest beers.

Roasted barley: An unmalted, roasted six-row barley that is roasted to a dark, almost black colour. Lends a dark color and coffee flavor ideal for porters and stouts. EBC typically over 1,000

Wheat malt: Not all malts are from Barley. Wheat malt is quite common, giving a unique taste and just a small amount can help to retain a nice frothy head on your beer. Very pale colour, typically 3EBC. Can be used (obviously) for making wheat beer. I always add around 100grams to my recipes to help a good head.

Buying Malt

Your local home brew shop will likely stock the more common malts and grains that you need to make up your *grist* (the grains for the mash). If a recipe calls for one of the more specialist malts then one can usually find them on-line. The cheapest way to buy malt is in 25Kg sacks. I usually get my base malt (Marris Otter pale malt) in a 25KG sack which I then store inside a large airtight container in a cool, dark corner.

Malt will easily keep 6 months in this way, in my experience. The more speciality malts I will buy in smaller bags of perhaps just 1Kg or 500g.

Malted barley needs to be crushed (not ground) before being mashed. I tend to buy my grain ready crushed. For the best freshness most small suppliers and home brew shops will crush the malt only when you order it and then pack and ship. If you have the resources, then you can buy (or make) your own grain crusher which will allow you to buy un-crushed grains and crush it yourself just before mashing time. This also allows you some control over the 'fineness' of the crushing. Many believe that a finer crush is required for brew in a bag process.

Hops

There's a huge range of hops available to the home brewer these days, certainly in UK and USA this is true and probably many other countries also. The hops chosen for the beer you brew are probably the main influence on the taste of your beer when drinking.

The two main ingredients of hops that we are interested in are the *Alpha Acid* and the *Essential Oils*. It is the alpha acid that gives the bitter taste but only after it has been boiled for a considerable time to become isomerised.

Usually when you buy hops you will know the alpha acid content of that variety. Hops though, are subject to natural variations due to many factors. Hours of sunshine, average temperature, rainfall, picking time, drying process, etc. etc. Like wines, they vary from year to year and also will vary from one place to another, albeit to a lesser degree.

You will read elsewhere of formula and calculations that will calculate the bitterness (measured in IBUs, International Bitterness Units) resulting from boiling a given quantity of hops, for a certain length of time. These can be useful but are not as important or precise as many would make out. I tend to use the Alpha Acid content as a guide, particularly when following someone elses recipe.

For example if a recipe says to use 20 grams of a certain hop which has 9% AA and I have a similar hop but which has only 6%AA, then I would use 50% more of that hop, i.e. 30 grams, to give the same bittering effect as the original recipe.

Hops are generally described as *bittering hops* or *aroma hops*.

Bittering hops have been developed to yield a high alpha acid content and these hops nearly always go in at the start of the boil to get a full 90 minutes. On the other hand, aroma hops have been selected and developed for the tastes and smells that come from their essential oils.

Aroma hops are generally added later in the boil, when there is perhaps 20 minutes or less of boiling time. Some may be added right at the end of the boil, when the heat is turned off and the boil stops. This point is called *flame out*.

Even later hops are sometimes added after the wort has cooled somewhat, perhaps to around $80°C$.

Sometimes hops are added into the fermentation vessel after the initial fast fermenting has finished and the yeast is slowly finishing its job. This is referred to as 'Dry Hopping'.

With the huge variety of hops and the myriad possibilities for when to add them and how much to add, there is plenty of scope for experimentation to develop your beer exactly to your own taste.

In between the two groups of *bittering* and *aroma* hops are *Dual Purpose* hops. These are developed and marketed to be used as either bittering or aroma, perhaps even the same hop doing both functions. They tend to be hops with a mid-range alpha acidity and good flavour and aroma properties from their essential oils.

Hops are quite sensitive to the presence of oxygen in the air and also to light from sun or fluorescent lamps. They should be carefully stored. Most hop merchants to the home brewers will supply the hops vacuum packed in foiled bags. The vacuum keeping the oxygen away and the silver foiled bag keeping light away from the hops.

Many home brewers will keep their hop stocks in the freezer or a very cold fridge, just above freezing is reportedly the best temperature to use. If you buy a bag of hops and don't use the whole bag in a brew, it's best to keep the remainder in the bag, folded and rolled carefully to get as much air out as you can and then firmly closed, sellotape, bulldog clips, elastic bands and similar working reasonably well.

A vacuum sealer would be ideal as this sucks out most of the air from the bag, reducing the chance of oxygen getting to the precious hops. Over time the essential oils as well as the alpha acids will degrade.

Yeast

The last of the 4 main ingredients. The yeast you choose will have a noticeable effect on the taste of your beer.

There are many different strains of yeast from several different suppliers such as Fermentis, Danstar, White Labs. Many larger breweries will have their own strain of yeast which they have cultured over decades to get their prefered flavours and performance.

When you 'pitch' the yeast into your wort it needs to multiply very quickly to ensure that it is the dominant organism in there. To do this it will need the right temperature, sugars and oxygen. Boiling the wort will have driven the dissolved oxygen out of the wort and this is why it is important that the cooled wort is aerated vigorously before pitching the yeast.

Once the yeast has multiplied, and used up the dissolved oxygen in the wort it will continue to consume sugars and produce alcohol in anaerobic conditions with little, if any, oxygen required.

Some specialized yeasts may need continued support from oxygen and the fermenting wort my need rousing with a good shake or stirring with a sanitized spoon every couple of days during fermentation. If your brew has stopped fermenting but fermentation is not complete, as checked with a hydrometer, then often a good stir will rouse the yeast into action and it will finish its work.

There are two main groupings of yeast. These are *Top Fermenting* and *Bottom Fermenting*, the difference being the top fermenting yeasts tend to float near to the top of the wort.

Top fermenting yeasts have traditionally been mostly used in the production of British beers whereas European style lagers have tended to use bottom fermenting yeast.

As the yeast consumes the sugars, the level of alcohol in the liquid rises and eventually the point will come where the yeast will stop working. At this point it may only have consumed 80% of the fermentable sugars.

Some yeasts will consumer a higher proportion, leaving the finished beer more dry in taste, some yeasts will consume a lower proportion and hence a sweeter beer.

The percentage of fermentable sugars that are consumed under ideal condition is called the *attenuation rate* of the yeast. Choosing the right yeast for the beer you are trying to brew can clearly have an effect, more so on the sweetness of the beer but similarly, albeit to a lesser degree, on the alcohol content.

Yeasts are available to the home brewer in several forms. Simplest, and available from most home brew shops, are the sachets of pre-packed, dried yeasts.

Typically these contain 11.5g of yeast, enough for a 23Litre batch. Most home brew shops will carry at least a basic range of half a dozen of the most common dried yeasts.

Safale-04 for English Ales, Safale us-05 for American ales and IPAs, for example. These sachets are certainly the most convenient for the beginner home brewer. Mostly they don't need a starter and can simply be sprinkled onto the top of wort in the fermentation vessel. They are easily transported and so fine to get by mail order. They start fermentation very fast and are easy to store safely for a few months. I keep mine in the fridge.

A vastly wider range of yeast are available as *liquid yeast*. These will perform better than the dried sachet yeasts and add more interesting nuances to the beer you are trying to produce. Especially if you are trying to clone a particular beer and you know which strain of yeast is used by the brewery, an identical or very similar yeast will likely be available in liquid form.

Liquid yeast usually come in one of two forms of packaging. In a sealed tube/vial is usually cheaper and has the right strain of healthy yeast inside. However there is generally not sufficient to ferment 23 Litre batch and so this must be made into a starter to grow more yeast.

The other form is in a 'smack pack' which has the yeast and nutrient inside, but in separate containers. Giving the pack a good smack with the hand will rupture the internal packing and allow the two solutions to mix. As the yeast multiplies, the bag will swell due to the CO_2 being generated. When ready just pitch into the wort.

Temperature of the wort during fermentation is quite important to keep under control. Most yeast work best at around 18°C - 20°C, specialised lager yeasts often work better at lower temperatures. The ideal working temperature will be noted on the packaging of the yeast. Too cold and the yeast may weaken and not finish the fermentation, too warm and off flavours can soon develop.

Adapting a Recipe

There are many recipes available from more experienced brewers for 'all grain' brewing, in books and on the internet. Many of them will have been developed to clone a particular brand of beer. Most of these recipes will be intended for brewing using the traditional 3 vessel all grain brewing method where the mashing and sparging will be done in a *Mash* Tun and then the wort transferred into the kettle for boiling.

Very little, if anything, needs to change from the recipe for BIAB brewing. BIAB will start with all the water used being in the kettle at the beginning so I simply look for the line in the recipe that indicates *Total Liquor* and use that as my starting quantity of water.

Each brewer's process and equipment will likely vary a little and so whichever method is used, there will be some small differences in the result. Perhaps the OG will be a little lower, or the final volume into the FV will be a little higher. This is commonly as a result of different *efficiency* of the process. The efficiency being how effective the process is at getting the available sugars out of the grains.

Sometimes a note with the recipe will say something along the lines of *"Based on an efficiency of 78%"* . As you make your first few brews and record results you will be able to calculate your own process efficiency. You may then decide to adjust recipes to take into account your own efficiency. If your process is less efficient, you'd increase the quantities of grains, for example, to allow for this.

Software

After brewing using other people's recipes you'll more than likely want to develop your own recipe. This can be done with trial and error, tweaking the hop additions perhaps, or adding some specialty malt.

Keeping good notes of the changes you make and the features of the beer that results will help immensely with this.

Calculations can be done to give a reasonable forecast of the colour of the beer, the bitterness (IBUs) and the alcohol content (ABV) before you even start the brewing. I won't discuss these calculations as that is really beyond the scope of this book, there is plenty of reference on the internet for this.

These calculations can be simplified with a spreadsheet or even simpler, there are many software packages available that will do these for you.

There are some very simple ones that make reasonable assumptions about the equipment and process that you will use. There are also extremely detailed and complete packages that will all fine tuning of all the parameters of your own equipment and process, will hold a database of all available grains, yeasts, hops, etc with water treatment calculators and other 'bells and whistles'.

These days there are also available good software apps that will run on a smart-phone, with in-built timers and alarms to awaken you once mashing is finished or other important stages. Also there are plenty of on-line recipe calculators that also work quite well.

I use Graham Wheelers 'Beer Engine' software to work out my recipe. This is written for the Windows operating system but installs and runs just fine in Linux (my PC runs Linux). This is completely free to download and use and has a quite simple interface.

A few days before I plan a brew I'll run the software, experiment with the quantities, and check that it is meeting my targets for ABV, bitterness and colour. Also I'll keep an eye on the Total Liquor it is forecasting will be needed.

If it is a particularly strong beer I am aiming for, the total liquor may be more than I can accommodate in my pot, in which case I could probably reduce the target finished quantity from 23 litres to, maybe 20 litres.

Some of the more commonly used software packages include:-

Beersmith

Available on most platforms PC, Mac, Android. A truly professional package supported with forums, podcasts, blogs, weekly newsletter etc. 21 day free trial to see if you like it. Available from www.beersmith.com.

Brewers Friend.

A free program for windows. Available from www.brewersfriend.com

There is a wonderful on-line resource for BIAB brewers at www.biabbrewer.info

On that site members can download for free an excel spreadsheet developed especially for BIAB brewing. It looks quite complex, but many use it regularly once they have understood how to use it.

Mashing

Mashing can be simple or complicated. In keeping with BIAB principles I tend to keep it very simple, using just two temperature steps. However, if you wish, even more control over the finished product can be gained by starting the mashing at a lower temperature and raising the temperature in 'steps' often called rests, to allow different enzymes to act on the barley in different ways.

Some brewers, for example, would start with a *protein rest* by doughing in at 50°C for 15 minutes and then increase the temperature to 66°C for the main mash. This initial step would allow proteolytic enzymes to break down some of the proteins in the malt and may be useful if you are brewing a particularly pale lager which you like to drink really cold.
Proteins in your finished beer are the main cause of *chill haze* which is a cloudy appearance that develops when beer is served very cold.

Most malted barleys available as base malts for brewing these days are modified to reduce the available proteins and so I feel this step is unnecessary, especially for darker bitters, porters, stouts, etc..

The main two enzymes in the malt that we use for the mashing are the *Beta Amylase* and the *Alpha Amylase*. These both need to be working on dissolved starches (hence the water). They both work best when the water is slightly acid.

Beta Amylase is most effective with a pH value of between 5.0 and 5.5 whereas the Alpha Amylase prefers slight less acidity in the water with with a pH value of between 5.2 and 5.7.

Consequently we aim for a pH value that suits both of these at 5.3pH. I will typically check the pH of my mash about 15 minutes after it has started.

I use litmus test strips and after giving the mash a good stir will take a large spoon full of the liquid from the pot and put on a white saucer. Then dip the strip for a few seconds. The acidity changes the colour of the central test zone on the strip and adjacent comparison colours allow me to compare and determine the pH of the mash.

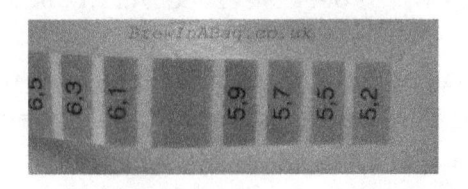

More advanced brewers would possibly use an electronic pH meter which can be purchased quite economically these days. However, I'm not so confidant of the accuracy of the cheaper models and even a professional one will need calibrating with solutions of know acidity before use and I understand that the pH sensor itself has a rather limited life.

Once mashing is started, there is nothing that can be usefully done to change the pH. The reading is noted so that if it is not in the correct range, then adjustments can be made to the liquor the next time I brew a similar batch. I'm possibly lucky with my water, but have never found my pH to be out of the target range.

Temperature is a key variable during the mash, as mentioned in this section and earlier. The Beta Amylase is most active at between $60°^C$ and $63°^C$. The Alpha Amylase is most active at between $68°^C$ and $70°^C$. In between these ranges, both are still actively working to convert starches to sugars.

For a single step mash, most brewers aim for a target temperature of $66°^C$ and try and maintain this for an hour or more.

Alpha is producing mainly fermentable sugars, beta is producing mainly un-fermentable sugars. You can therefore understand how adjusting your mashing temperature can have a significant effect on your finished beer.

A lower mashing temperature will give mainly fermentable sugars and therefore potentially higher alcohol content and a drier, crisp taste with little residual sweetness. Conversely, higher mashing temperatures would give a greater proportion of non-fermentable sugars resulting in lower alcohol content and a sweeter beer with more *'body'*.

Generally if the pH and temperatures are right, then mashing is pretty much finished in 45 minutes or so. A little longer does no harm and I usually mash at 66°^{C} for around 75 minutes. I then check that all the starches have been converted. Iodine has a very useful property when in solution. If it comes into contact with starch it stains it a very dark black colour.

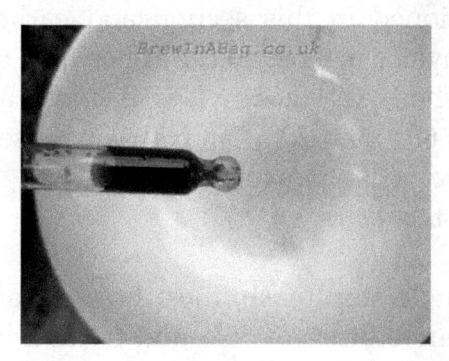

I use a small bottle of Lugols Iodine, available from health food shops, pharmacists, and on-line. After stirring the mash, I put a large spoonful of liquid from the mash into a shallow plain white bowl and drip just one drop of the iodine solution into the liquid. If it turns black, then there are still starches present, I'll let the mash run another 15 minutes and test again.

This is not something I practise with each brew I make, only for a beer I'm brewing for the first time.

When I am happy that the mash is complete, the next stage is called *Mash Out* and this involves raising the temperature to above 76°C. This will denature the enzymes and halt their activity. I lift the bag to make sure that it is not touching the bottom of the kettle, leave it hanging there on the chord & pulley. Then on with the gas, at 76°C, lower the bag, good stir for five minutes or so before lifting the bag fully out to drain.

Boiling

Up until this point, things have needed to be kep clean, but not completely sanitised as any bacteria in the wort will be killed off by boiling for an hour. From now on though, anything that will contact the wort will need to be sterilised. The boiling of the sweet wort was the main factor that made beer such a healthy drink long before the notions of bacteria and infection were considered.

The boiling process is where the hops are generally added. Hops contain alpha *acids* and when these are isomerised, they give the beer the distinctive bitter taste of the hops. The process of isomerisation takes time and temperature to be fully effective.

At the start of boil, the bittering hops are added and these are generally boiled for 90 minutes to fully isomerise the alpha acids.

A few minutes into the boil a thick foam will generally start to form on the top of the liquid. If you don't have much 'head space' in your boiler this may well spill over and make a nasty sticky mess down the side of the boiler and spreading around wherever it is not wanted.

This is known as a boil-over and all home brewers have suffered at least one in their time and possibly several more. The foam can be dispersed by spraying a fine mist of water onto it with a spray bottle and you should probably turn down the heat as soon as this happens.

This foam is known as the *Hot Break* and is important to get this. Within the wort are dissolved proteins and you want to keep these out of your finished beer. Dissolved proteins are the main cause of hazy beer, particularly *Chill Haze* which occurs when a wonderfully clear beer becomes cloudy when cooled in a fridge.

The hot break occurs when the proteins come out of solution and begin to clump together (*Flocculate*).

It is important to keep the top of the boiler open, with no lid. Malting grain produces chemicals including Dimethyl sulphide (DMS) and similar, sulphur containing chemicals. These will give an unwanted taste to the beer and need to be removed. During a good vigorous boil, they will be driven off and carried away with the steam.

There is going to be a lot of steam generated during a 90 minute boil and this is one of the main problems with brewing indoors. It is quite possible that 10% of your water will evaporate as steam during the boil and this will condense in all sorts of places around your room(s).

Obvious measures can be taken to remove this, extractor fans, open windows etc, but don't be tempted to keep a lid on the boiler to try and contain this steam as the DMS will condense with the water and drip back into the wort.

About 30 minutes into the boil, if your bag is still hanging over the pot, it will have drained pretty much all it is likely to release under its own weight. At this point many will remove the bag, I prefer to extract as much goodness as I can and so will squeeze the bag using a couple of flat saucepan lids (to keep the HOT, sticky wort off my hands) and get around another litre out of the grain.

There is a lot of debate about 'to squeeze - or not to squeeze' with some saying it will extract extra tannins from the grain, and they may be right but I have not noticed this effect.

Late Addition hops are those which are added later in the process. Recipes will tell you when to add them and this will be defined in minutes from *Flameout*, the term used to describe the moment when boiling is stopped.

The late addition hops will give the beer flavour and aroma. With, typically, ten minutes or less of boiling, the essential oils and beta acids will be released into the wort and are less likely to be boiled off.

Many will add hops at ten minutes from the end, perhaps also at flameout itself and sometimes a short while after flameout when the wort temperature has dropped to 80°C.

At around 10 minutes from flameout, I rinse off my *Immersion Wort Chiller,* which will help cool the wort, and lower it into the wort. By boiling it for 10 minutes this will ensure it is sanitised.

I will also get my glass jug and run off a jugful of wort through the tap into the jug and pour this back into the kettle. I'll do this a few times which will sanitise the tap and pipe and the jug.

This is the time also to add a part of a *Protafloc* tablet. This is *Irish Moss* in tablet form. Irish moss acts as a flocculant and works really well to help the proteins and other unwanted bits in the wort to clump together ready for sinking to the bottom and filtering out. A quarter of a tablet is usually enough for a 23 Litre batch of wort. Ten to fifteen minutes of boiling is enough time for that.

Cooling

Once the boil is finished then it is necessary to cool the wort to *Pitching* Temperature as quickly as possible. The warm sugary wort is ideal breeding ground for bacteria so I like to get it cool and the yeast pitched as quickly as possible to help reduce the chance of an infection.

Additionally, rapid cooling will encourage the *Cold Break* another opportunity for the proteins to clump together and settle. DMS, which we have mostly been driven out during the boil, will start to re-form whilst the wort is hot so cooling quickly will also reduce DMS levels.

I use a simple immersion chiller that I made myself, quite simply. This is merely a 10m length of 10mm diameter copper central heating tube, that I formed into a coil by wrapping around a wine fermenting demijohn although almost any cylinder of around 8 inches diameter would do as a former.

Before immersing it in the wort I clip my garden hose on with a jubilee clip and another short length of hose pipe at the other end to take away the water to drain.

Once I turn the hose on, cold water goes into the chiller and draws heat from the wort. The water coming out of the chiller is, at first, very hot, certainly hot enough to scold your skin so be careful when it is first turned on.

With the wort chiller in the boiler, I put on the lid as best as I can to try and keep things out of the beer. The chiller will cool the wort to below 30°C in around 30 minutes.

An alternative to using a chiller is to put the boiler full of wort into an ice bath.

Many indoor brewers will use the bath-tub for this with cold water and ice-cubes or pre-frozen plastic bottles of water for cooling.

A large kitchen sink can often do the same job, with the cold tap left running into the sink at a rate sufficient to match the draining of the water through the overflow.

Whilst more expensive and possibly more difficult to clean, a multiplate chiller (heat exchanger) is used by some. This has an inlet pipe for cold water, an outlet for the resulting heated water. The wort also flows through this chiller through another pair of inlet/outlets, but is separated from the cooling water by the plates. These are very effective at rapidly cooling the wort.

Some would say they allow the clumped proteins from the cold break to make their way into the fermenting vessel and they are not so easy to thoroughly sanitise. Nevertheless, the benefits of very fast cooling in just the time it takes to drain from boiler to FV make these devices popular. Clearly those brewers that use them are very satisfied with the result.

Of increasing popularity is the *No-Chill* method of cooling. In this method, a container that is just sufficient to hold all of the wort, is filled as soon as practical after flameout.

This means the wort going into the container is hot enough to pasteurise the inside of the container and prevent bacterial infection.

Containers are usually a suitably food-safe plastic. Once the hot wort is in the container the lid is tightly fitted and the container is shaken to make sure all internal surfaces are sanitised. The wort can then be left overnight to cool and then transferred to the fermentation vessel the next day, or perhaps even a few days later. This can be very convenient.

Whichever method is chosen for cooling the wort it is a good idea to take a sample of the boiled wort so that the specific gravity can be measured. Check the temperature of your sample when measuring the S.G. and correct if different to that for which your hydrometer is calibrated.

When the wort is cool enough it should be transferred into the sanitised Fermenting Vessel.

During the 30 or so minutes that mine is cooling, the clumped together proteins and grain flour and hops will have sunk to the bottom of the boiler. The hops will form an effective filter to catch the Cold Break material. I'll open the tap for a moderate flow and fill the previously sanitised jug. This will be very carefully poured back into the top and this repeated 3 or 4 times until the hops are working well as a filter and the wort flows clear.

If your boil pot has not drain tap then one can pour the wort into the fermenting vessel through a sanitised sieve or syphon the wort into the FV using a sanitised syphon tube.

Through most of the process, before and after this point, it is a bad idea to get air (Oxygen) into your wort. However, during the early part of the fermentation the yeast needs some oxygen so plenty of splashing of the wort into the FV is a good idea.

Fermenting

Fermentation is the process of yeast cells consuming the sugars and splitting them into alcohol and carbon dioxide. There are three main stages to the fermentation. Initially there will some lag during which the cells are multiplying, this may be up to 24 hours.

In this stage they are consuming dissolved oxygen from the wort. This stage is when the wort is most susceptible to infection and so it is much better if this stage can be kept as short as possible.

Generally ale yeasts (top fermenting) prefer to be at around $18°^C$ - $20°^C$ but I pitch my yeast when the wort is warmer than this, at anything between $20°^C$ and $30°^C$, to encourage the yeast to get off to a good start and try and reduce the lag time.

I'll start cooling the wort at this time also so that after 24 hours it is at $20°^C$, considerably lower, perhaps $15°^C$, if using a bottom fermenting lager yeast.

The second stage is when most of the conversion is done. 24 hours after pitching the yeast should have produced a good thick *Krausen* on the top of the wort.

The Krausen is a thick foam mixture of yeast and protein bubbles, typically off-white in colour with brown yeast mixed among it and particles of grain or grain flower called *trub* and pronounced troob.

If you have a suitable fermenting vessel to allow access, then the top layer of this could be skimmed off with a sanitised spoon to aid clarity in your final beer.

If you have an airlock on your fermenting vessel you will notice very rapid bubbling, a bubble every second or two, perhaps more.

Out of interest I kept a regular check on the bubbling rate of one of my brews, not very scientific, I know, but interesting.

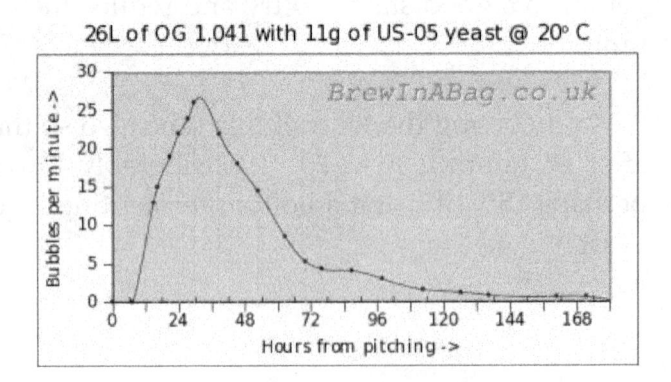

26L of OG 1.041 with 11g of US-05 yeast @ 20° C

The bubbling rate is only an indication of the whats happening. During this time the conversion is happening and as well as the alcohol and CO_2, there are other chemicals being produced, many of which the yeast will clear up in the final stage, secondary fermentation.

I find primary fermentation is typically finished within 7 - 10 days, you can see from the above chart that bubbling had stopped on the seventh day.

Most of this time, the Maltose is being consumed by the yeast, but probably by the fourth or fifth day these will have been totally consumed, then, it is the less fermentable sugars, some of the Dextrins, that are being slowly converted.

Sometimes this will be shorter time and fermentation rate can typically be shortened by fermenting at a higher temperature.

However, do not by tempted to deliberately ferment at a higher temperature as 'off' flavours can be caused. In primary fermentation, patience is certainly a virtue.

During the main stage of primary fermentation, it is important to keep the fermentation proceeding in the right temperature range and also at a fairly constant temperature.

Many home brewers will have constructed an insulated place to do the fermentation, probably with temperature control, and a suitably sized refrigerator is often put to this task.

With the shelves removed, and a suitable stand for the F.V., a heat pad or small oil filled heater, or even an incandescent light bulb of around 100W rating below the F.V. would be used.

If the temperature drops too low the heat source turns on and the fridge mechanism itself turned on instead if the temperature rises too high. Often these are controlled with a simple PID controller such as the STC1000 commonly available on the internet.

The best way to be sure that the primary fermentation is finished is by measuring the specific gravity daily once you think it may have finished.

I use a sanitised Turkey Baster to extract some wort from the fermenting vessel and transfer it into a sample jar to take the gravity reading.

If the SG is within a couple of points of the target final gravity AND it has remained unchanged for 24 hours then primary fermentation has finished.

If fermentation seems to have stopped but the SG is more than 2 points above the theoretical target, then the yeast may need to be re-awoken to finish its job. A good slow stir with a properly sanitised spoon should do the trick. Try to stir up the yeast from the bottom of the FV. Try also to stir in a manner that will minimise aeration for, at this point, extra oxygen in the wort is not a good idea.

Conditioning

After fermentation is complete, the beer should be transferred into another vessel for conditioning. Many will use another, sanitised fermenting vessel and keep the beer in that for 2 or 3 days before bottling or transferring to a keg or a cask.

Some will add a fining agent which helps and remaining yeast sink to the bottom and clarify the beer.

Gelatine is popular, very effective and cheap to buy. Isinglass is another commonly used fining agent which does the same job, using smaller quantities. Neither of these add any noticable flavour to the beer.

I nearly always use a commercially available plastic pressure barrel and transfer the beer directly to that from the F.V. The brand name I use is King Keg, but there are certainly others available.:-

This holds up to 25 Litres and has a high level tap, connected behind with a flexible pipe to a float so that beer is always drawn from just below the surface.

The high tap makes it easy to fill a glass, even if the keg is on the floor or at the back of a shelf. I prime with around 100g of regular white sugar and then siphon the beer from the FV into the keg, making sure to keep the output of the siphon tube below the surface in the keg to avoid aeration.

This needs to be kept somewhere warm, around 20°C, for a week to allow the yeast to continue its final clearing up, and then settle to the bottom. Then I'll move the keg somewhere cool, and in the summer this means my fridge, and keep the beer at around 10°C for serving (Ale) or perhaps lower at around 6°C or 7°C for a lager.

After a week in the cool temperature, I will sometimes then bottle the beer into sterilised dark brown bottles. Any bottles you use must have been manufactured suitable for containing the pressure that a beer has.

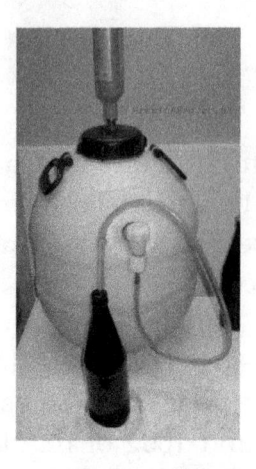

Even with purpose made glass beer bottles, check them carefully for chips and cracks and discard those which are not in good condition.

Although the beer has conditioned well in the KingKeg and is carbonated (fizzy) I will add a half teaspoon of plain white sugar to each bottle before filling with the beer. This will allow the yeast to generate some more CO_2 whilst in the bottle to ensure the beer is not flat when opening.

Jargon List

ABV
Alcohol by volume.

Attenuation
Refers to yeast and how effective it is at converting sugars to alcohols.

DP
Diastatic Power. The strength in the malt enzymes for converting starch to sugar.

Doughing-In
Mixing the grains into the water at the start of mashing.

FG
Final Gravity. The specific gravity of the beer when fermentation is finished.

Flameout
The point at the end of boiling when the heat is turned off.

FV
Fermenting Vessel

Hot Break
During the boil, proteins come out of solution and clump together.

Kettle
The vessel which is used for boiling the wort, sometimes called the copper.

Liquor
The water, sometimes treated, used to mash the grains.

Mash
The process of soaking the grains in warm water (approx 66°C)

Mash Tun
Separate vessel, with filtering and insulation just for mashing and sparging.

OG
Original Gravity. The specific gravity of the wort before fermentation.

Pitching
Adding the yeast to the wort to begin fermentation.

Strike
Strike temperature is the temp of the water before adding the grains.

Wort
The sweet liquid that drains from the mashed grains.

Useful Tables

Temperature Correction Table for 20 Degree Hydrometer.

Temp °C	Correction
12°C	-.0013
14°C	-.0010
16°C	-.0007
18°C	-.0004
20°C	0
22°C	+.0004
24°C	+.0007
26°C	+.0014
28°C	+.0020
30°C	+.0026
32°C	+.0032
34°C	+.0039
36°C	+.0045
38°C	+.0053
40°C	+.0060
42°C	+.0068

Temperature Conversion

Centigrade	Fahrenheit
20	68
25	77
30	86
35	95
40	104
45	113
50	122
55	131
60	140
65	149
70	158
75	167
80	176
85	185
90	194
95	203
100	212